PREDICTIONS

BY THE SAME AUTHOR

Population

JOHN I. CLARKE

PHŒNIX

A PHOENIX PAPERBACK

First published in Great Britain in 1997 by
Phoenix, a division of the Orion Publishing Group Ltd
Orion House
5 Upper Saint Martin's Lane
London, WC2H 9EA

A CIP catalogue record for this book is available
from the British Library.

ISBN 0 297 81923 2

Typeset by SetSystems Ltd, Saffron Walden
Set in 9/13.5 Stone Serif
Printed in Great Britain by
Clays Ltd, St Ives plc.

Contents

Predictions and Projections

Seen within the continuity of time, the year 2000 is probably no more likely than any other year to be a significant threshold, certainly for population changes. And yet for many people it has been a target for living, working and forecasting, a focus for opportunities for change, and a launch-pad for the future, so its significance must not be ruled out. What a damp squib if our dreams of millennial change prove to be no more radical than the social, moral and artistic ripples of the *fin de siècle* movement at the end of the nineteenth century. Many of us dream that we can improve our age by tackling its spectres: environmental degradation, poverty, inequality and the spectre which some over the last half-century have considered at the root of all the others, population growth. But can we be sure that it will remain a key concern far into the next century?

Predictions in the Social Sciences

Predictions and forecasts trip easily off our tongues, but we are rarely accountable for their accuracy. Predictions of human systems are generally more difficult than those of physical systems, because they obey fewer laws and tend to change more rapidly. Hence social scientists tread cautiously and sometimes actively avoid predictions, as they smack of pseudo-science and Nostradamus. Futurology has never really taken off, but the fogginess of the future must not deter us from peering into it. Forecasting has been called an impossible but unavoidable task.

Like most social scientists, demographers are much

better at explaining the past and the present of populations than predicting their future – they are better at backcasting than forecasting. Even explaining the revolutionary changes that have occurred during the twentieth century is a formidable task, let alone speculating about the more revolutionary changes that will take place during the next century. Indeed, for fear of being considered unscientific, demographers usually say that they don't make predictions or forecasts of future populations; they only make projections based upon collected data and existing trends. Population projections may not escape the scepticism of cynics, but they do encompass the elements of uncertainty. In a sense, projections are conditional (rather than unconditional) predictions, which assume certain external events. Nevertheless, demographers are none too keen on making them, not only because they are shots in the dark, but also because they are frequently misinterpreted. They cannot escape the challenge, however, because governments require projections for planning, and they are also needed by many other institutions to assess the consequences of population change. Above all, the alarming speed of world population growth from 2.5 billion at mid-century to nearly 6 billion now has made global projections a necessity.

The Problem of Population Projections

Projections are statistical computations about future population size and characteristics, based upon assumptions about the three main components of population change: births, deaths and migration. Best calculated for the short term of twenty to thirty years, they do not claim high levels of accuracy over the long term, say fifty to a hundred years. The chances of accuracy are much greater for the short term, because people who will be over twenty to thirty are already born, and their numbers will be reduced only by the death rate, which is fairly stable, or (in local populations) by out-migration, which is highly variable. These people will be the main reproductive age-groups, so if we exclude migration the main problem is to estimate their rate of future child-bearing. That is why current projections rarely go beyond 2025 or 2030 with any degree of confidence – well within the lifetime of most people living today. Projections for the longer term are much more speculative as they depend much more on guesses about births. Those for the year 2100, which are now frequently made for the world population as a whole, will include only a tiny number of today's infants who survive as centenarians and who might be able to check on their validity. Unless we are seriously wrong about human longevity and there are totally unforeseen changes in store, nobody will be still around to check the current global projections for the year 2150.

A useful analogy has been made that the demographer making population projections is rather like a car-driver, who knows something about the situation in hand, but thereafter has to make modifications according to acceleration, obstacles or special conditions. The near future of populations is seen much better than the distant future, partly because it is more dependent upon the population size and characteristics of the present and recent past. We should also note that the long-term past has less influence on the future, and that there is a real danger in going back too far to predict the long-term future. For example, it is inappropriate to consider the so-called 'exponential growth' of world population over the past two centuries to project the world population of future centuries. Rather than continuity of past trends, it is much more likely that there will be unforeseen future fluctuations and discontinuities.

Populations are located within physical and human environments that are constantly changing, and it is less and less easy to consider populations in isolation from other factors, such as the environment, energy and food supply. Populations are influenced by all manner of major and minor processes and events, the processes being usually easier to envisage than the events. With no experimental data to go on, demographers have merely been able to project numerically past or current population trends, being unaware of the possible impact of major physical, social, technological, economic and political discontinuities or shifts, which may have enormous effects on population numbers and movements. Examples from the last few decades are the introduction of the contraceptive pill, the spread of AIDS, dramatic demographic changes in China, Third World conflicts leading to massive refugee movements, the proliferation of air travel, the effect of the microchip upon communications, the rapidly rising status of women in many countries, and the break-up of the Soviet Union. Some are beginnings, some are endings. All were largely unforeseen, but are having immense repercussions upon populations.

Indeed, if we think of the six-fold multiplication of world population during the nineteenth and twentieth centuries from one billion to over six billion, we will recall that it was greatly influenced by many non-demographic discontinuities, including the industrial, agricultural and transport revolutions, the diffusion of European colonialism and nationalism, major medical and educational advances, almost ubiquitous urbanization, the huge growth of large cities, the mercurial rise of the service sector and the ever increasing rapidity of modern communications. Few of these great changes were within sight of long-term prediction two centuries ago, even by a genius like Thomas Robert Malthus, who first published his classic *An essay on the principle of population as it affects the future improvement of society* in 1798. So we must not expect too much from our projections.

Unfortunately, whether demographers like it or not, their projections are often taken to be predictions or forecasts by the many governments, companies, environmentalists and others, who are all searching for the best available estimates of future populations. Environmentalists, for example, have applied them in their concerns about the increasing impact of rising populations upon the environment, a matter to which demographers had given relatively little attention until recently. The mere fact that population projections are presented as numbers means that they are often awarded an unwarranted degree of accuracy and credibility by the general public. Numbers give projections viability. Acceptance and use of projections as unconditional predictions is all the more likely if they are made by well-known official bodies such as the United Nations Population Division and the World Bank.

Past Projections

The historical record of population projections is not littered with successes, but it has improved greatly in recent decades. We have come a long way from the first recorded long-term projection of world population by Gregory King in 1696, who stated that 'if the World should continue to [anno mundi] 20,000 [AD 16,052] it might then have 6,500 million', no doubt an extraordinary total to him, but one which should be achieved during the early years of the twenty-first century. He merely applied an estimated growth rate to an estimated population size. A simple method, it was widely used well into the twentieth century, although its value for the long term was strictly limited. During the years between the two world wars, G. H. Knibbs (1928) used a similar approach to long-term global projection, giving a total for AD 2000 less than two-thirds of the now expected reality.

About the same time, Raymond Pearl and Lowell J. Read

were using a more biological approach based upon the mathematical form of the S-shaped logistic curve. It assumed that the rate of growth is a linearly decreasing function of population size, and that there are cycles of population growth reflecting changes in the economic organization of society and in the population densities that can be sustained. Devised from studies of yeast cells and fruit flies, it supported Malthusian theory that population growth would right itself by its own checks. Consequently, Pearl's 1924 projection of world population did not envisage the enormous subsequent growth, and gave a total for the year 2000 less than one-third of what is now expected. The logistic curve, which found favour among many ecologists, was later used by others for human populations, but with disappointing results, and it has since been overtaken by better techniques.

Some of the projections made for developed countries before and immediately after the Second World War have proved very inaccurate. Many countries feared that there would be a continued decline in the birth rate and made assumptions accordingly. Such fear of population decline was epitomized by Enid Charles' book *The Twilight of Parenthood* (1934). Thus Eva Hubback's 1947 projections for the population of England and Wales in 1989 were only 33–37 million, hopelessly inaccurate when the total actually attained was well over 50 million. Equally, UK government projections made in 1955 for 1995 were still many millions below the later reality. In France and many other developed countries, the virtues of large families were extolled to overcome fears of population decline.

Improved Projections
Curiously, since the middle of the twentieth century, when the world population began to grow at an unprecedented rate, projections have improved markedly, largely because

of progress in population theory and methods, and because of a huge increase in the availability and quality of population data.

Improvements in theory and methods owe much to the work of Frank Notestein and his colleagues, who in 1944 presented population projections for Europe and the Soviet Union using the cohort component method that projects populations by age and sex cohorts. In the following year, he and his colleagues produced the first modern projections of the world population. Although he arrived at a world total of only 3.3 billion people for the year 2000, a total actually achieved by the mid-1960s, his approach was seminal. It was based upon 'demographic transition theory' – the way that populations evolve from pre-modern high fertility and mortality (the incidence of births and deaths) to post-modern low fertility and mortality, and from slow growth through phases of rapid growth to slow growth again – with separate assessments of age–sex structures and separate assumptions about the incidence of births, deaths and migration for national and regional populations. These assumptions are of course critical and always a matter of debate. Fairly precise data about age and sex structures are also a necessary basis for the projections. Generally, three sets of projections have been made – 'high', 'medium' (that is, most likely) and 'low' variants – although the reasoning behind the assumptions for these variants has not always been made clear. Nevertheless, the method was widely accepted and was subsequently used for a whole series of projections, which took us a step nearer to understanding our demographic future.

In the 1950s and 1960s the United Nations made a series of global projections for the year 2000 which have proved to be remarkably near the mark, even if the regional breakdown has been less accurate. For instance, the 1957 medium projection indicated a total of 6.3 billion for 2000, slightly above our current expectations; we now believe that 6 billion will be attained in 1999 as the total is increasing by just under 1.5 per cent or 81 million a year, but that increase is going down all the time, and projections are being modified accordingly. Not surprisingly, a successive record of realistic world projections by the United Nations has inspired considerable confidence. Consequently, its 1992 medium projection of 8.5 billion for 2025 was widely accepted as reasonable (although the World Bank figure was lower at 8.35 billion and that of the International Institute for Applied Systems Analysis (IIASA) in Austria higher at 8.96 billion), but later projections are lower.

Such confidence should certainly be tempered when considering the United Nations 1992 long-range projections for 1950–2150, and we should be very wary of accepting without caution its median estimate of 11.54 billion for the world population in the year 2150, especially when we realize that its low estimate is 4.29 billion and its high estimate is 28.02 billion. With such a huge range, the projections merely tell us that anything is possible, and their credibility disappears. Faced with requests for dates when world population will stabilize and for projections comparable with those of global environmental change (which is scientifically more predictable than global population change), perhaps demographers have been inveigled too much into making long-term projections.

Since the 1970s, this cohort component method has been extended by the preparation of scenario projections, which make clear-cut assumptions about fertility, mortality and migration. Scenario projections are principally policy-making tools aimed at facilitating demographic transition to low fertility and mortality rather than at defining future population trends as accurately as possible. Essentially, the scenario approach is concerned with demonstrating what will happen to population if certain component rates prevail. Consequently, a variety of scenarios is presented for subsequent analysis, showing not only the probable population changes but also the range of possibilities if certain social behaviours persist. A recent example is that by Wolfgang Lutz (1994) and colleagues at IIASA, who presented nine scenarios, including a central middle-of-the-road scenario, for their long-term projections of world population until the year 2100.

Whatever the projections, they have mainly focused on future numbers and age–sex structures rather than on future spatial patterns, movements and inequalities, which are of great importance to the people on the ground, whether they are policy-makers or citizens. Spatial considerations have attracted less attention from demographers, except those areal units used for census enumerations. On the other hand, a group of spatial demographers and population geographers have made considerable advances in the specialized modelling of spatial populations. Their multiregional projections are based on complex matrices combining the effects of natural change and of inward and outward migration (rather than the balance – net migration). Unfortunately, while they are valuable theoretically they are difficult to apply. Single region projections are more common but conceptually more restricted; they are based less on the interdependence of regions and more on how local phenomena rather than national averages would influence population change in a specific region. The real difficulty in these projections is in incorporating the effects of striking geographical diversity upon population dynamics.

Projections are not done in isolation. Numerous

attempts have been made to relate population projections to quantifiable economic and environmental phenomena such as food supplies, production, specific natural resources (of water, forests, fish stocks, minerals, soils etc), land-use changes and pollution, all of which will in turn affect future numbers of people. Alone, population numbers are not very meaningful.

Better Data

The second reason for improvements in projections over the second half of the twentieth century is the great growth and improved quality of population data. While most developed countries and a few less developed countries (for example, India, Algeria and Egypt) started census-taking during the nineteenth century, many less developed countries, most notably China and many African countries, have undertaken modern censuses only since mid-century. Under the aegis of the United Nations, census-taking and sample surveys have expanded to nearly all of the countries in the world, enabling many newly independent states to find out their population numbers for the first time, conferring upon these states a sort of demographic legitimacy. Each decennial round has seen improvements, although censuses vary immensely in accuracy, periodicity, comprehensiveness and content, and tend to be more reliable in richer than in poorer countries. Many are far from perfect, even in developed countries, and often ethnic and political issues interfere with accuracy. For instance, the Afro-American and illegal immigrant populations of the United States are usually under-enumerated by millions, and in the United Kingdom about 1 million of the 58 million inhabitants 'went missing' at the time of the 1991 census, probably because of the proposed introduction of the poll tax. Less developed countries have even exaggerated population numbers to attract aid or prestige. Good censuses are indispensable to good government, and a top priority for the future.

There have been no comparable improvements in civil registration (vital registration of births, marriages and deaths, and population registers) and in recording the manifold movements of migrants. The accuracy of registration of vital events and movements leaves much to be desired, particularly because it is too expensive for many poorer countries where bureaucracies are often either inadequate or resented. This is in spite of the fact that present populations are generally much better educated than in the early days of vital registration in the developed countries during the nineteenth century. Fortunately, methods have been devised to analyse incomplete data, and the World Fertility Survey (WFS) held in sixty-two countries during 1974–86 and the Demographic and Health Surveys (DHS) which took place in a similar number of countries during 1986–95 have provided invaluable supplementary data.

On the whole, we can now have much more confidence in the current statistical basis from which regional and global projections are made. There is less guesswork about the baselines for projections. But sometimes projections have not reflected recent changes swiftly enough, as for example the slowing down of world population growth since the 1970s. Indeed, this fact is still not widely known, most of the public recalling a more rapid rate of population growth.

Except for the large-scale international surveys of fertility and health held in recent decades, there is still low international comparability of population data and great scope for improvement, especially at supra-national level. It is anomalous, to say the least, that while very high-resolution remote sensing is providing a global data set for land applications at a spatial resolution of 1 kilometre, only a few developed countries have produced comparable detailed geocoded data for populations. It is easier to map detailed environmental changes than population changes.

What Are Populations?

Populations of States

Most population censuses are national, and are founded on the concept of the modern state, which diffused remarkably around the world during the nineteenth and twentieth centuries, each state being endowed with a terrority over which it has sovereignty, a population, and a government authority with power to impose obligations. Enumeration of population is thus a political instrument. In many ways demography (the term was first used by Achille Guillard in 1855) started as political arithmetic, population data being collected by governments for the territories that they controlled and for their internal areal units: provinces, counties, districts, wards and so on.

Political boundaries of modern states have to a greater or lesser extent become demographic divides partitioning humanity. Their effectiveness varies over time and space. Some are formidable barriers, as between India and China and between the former East and West Germany, others are much more open, as between USA and Canada and between countries of the new European Union. In general, political boundaries have nationalized population problems, by preventing the free flow of people and by enabling governments to impose localized controls and policies concerning fertility and mortality. Both perpetuate the unevenness of world population distribution.

Everyone is required to be a citizen of a state, to have the nationality of a particular country. At international level, populations are generally distinguished by the territories in which they live, rather than as groups of people of ethnic, cultural or demographic identity, though such groups may be enumerated as sectoral or sub-populations (for example, linguistic, foreign, tribal, school, widowed populations). Central authority over a population with sovereignty over territory gives international recognition to a state. Hence, insistence on territorial integrity has been paramount. Sometimes its defence has led to the sacrifice of large numbers of citizens for small areas of land, yet the natural resources of a territory (such as minerals, water, wood) have been more or less freely exported, sometimes to the detriment of the citizens.

Ethnic Populations

Not all ethnic groups have a well-developed sense of territory – the gypsies are an example of one which doesn't – but there are many groups which wish to have sovereignty over particular territories with well-defined boundaries, and so to achieve recognition as populations and states. Governments have sometimes regarded their existence as a good enough reason to refrain from ethnic enumeration in a census, especially if the group is politically active or straddles political boundaries, like the Kurds, Palestinians and Basques. Extreme cultural diversity within a country, associated frequently with civil conflict, has been a factor in delaying census-taking in countries such as Afghanistan, Ethiopia and Lebanon, or in causing unreliable results, as in Nigeria, where the 1962 census proved so unacceptable that it was repeated in 1963 (and found another 10 million people). One joke of the time suggested that a census enumerator was someone who went from house to house increasing the population.

The current prevalence of ethnic, religious or linguistic groups increasingly expressing their desire for autonomy or independence is indicative of their uneasy accommodation within the modern system of centralized states, and challenges our accepted notion of a 'population'. This cannot fail to engender greater political concern as the uncertain future of the modern state unfolds. Either by formation or by current status, few states today are largely composed of a single ethnic group, although perhaps Japan has been able to lay a better claim than most. The boundaries of many new states, particularly in Africa, bear no relationship to ethnic distribution and diversity. Furthermore, international migrations have intensified ethnic and cultural diversity within states, especially the more developed ones, which have been the preferred destinations of most international migrants.

Many governments have made strenuous efforts to create nation-states from their diverse cultures, but it is an arduous, often intractable task in numerous newly independent countries. Often federal structures have been established to cope with the problem of internal diversity, but federalism has had varying levels of success around the world: the prolonged cohesion enjoyed by the United States, Brazil and India contrasts sharply with the recent fission of the former federal states of Yugoslavia and the Soviet Union. With almost three times as many independent states now as at the end of the Second World War, all the signs indicate continued formation of state populations in future decades. But will territorial sovereignty remain intrinsic to the state?

Globalization and International Groupings

The separateness of state populations is being constantly affected by external forces, most notably the impact of economic globalization and greater consciousness of a shared global environment with finite space and resources, easily damaged to the detriment of all. Among many other effects, globalization has widened the economic spectrum of countries and has provoked huge international migration of people and workers, usually from poorer to richer countries. This may be clearly exemplified in the Middle East by the massive demographic impact of the oil industry upon the Gulf States; some of the smaller states (for example, Kuwait, Arab Emirates, Bahrain, Qatar) have attracted so many migrant workers that they contain far more non-nationals than nationals. Just as states may encourage immigration, so they may choose at other times, such as during the Gulf War, to restrict or even reverse the flow. In recent years, some of the more populous developed countries of the West, faced with rising unemployment and severe competition from newly industrialized countries with cheaper labour, have been closing their doors to migrant workers. The global economy, as reflected in huge transnational companies establishing subsidiaries worldwide, may actively diminish the power of states and the distinctiveness of their populations. Countries cannot continue so easily to protect or perhaps control their own.

Economic globalization has not been accompanied by comparable political globalization. The United Nations has turned out to be only a loose grouping of states, far from a fusion of state populations or even a supra-national authority. At a practical level, however, it has had powerful direct and indirect effects upon state populations through its assistance in collecting data, training demographers, reducing fertility and mortality, improving health and education, and in helping migrants, notably refugees.

Conversely, one future powerful political force upon the population dynamics of states may well be the regional grouping of states, or even the emergence of regional states. The recent evolution of the European Union is expected to lead, for example, to increasing movements of people within its member states. Surely it will be emulated in some form elsewhere in the world, hopefully where new states have not yet proved to be very successful, either economically or politically, as in parts of Sub-Saharan Africa.

The space age, economic globalization, growing world population, regional inequalities and global environmental concerns have all encouraged more macro-level thinking about world regions and the world as a whole. Consequently, the statistical aggregation of state populations into supra-national demographic groupings (such as regional, continental, developed/less developed, global) for purposes of analysis and comparison has become commonplace. Inevitably, this involves considerable estimation, particularly for the world population, which Paul Demeny has called 'a figment of the statistician's imagination'. There are now well over 230 countries including dependencies (estimates vary depending on definitions of a 'country'), ranging in population from less than 10,000 inhabitants in some Caribbean and Pacific islands to over 1.2 billion in China, with population densities ranging from 1 to 5,000 per square kilometre and massive differences in population structures and dynamics, that do not lend themselves to simple aggregation.

With states having independent government policies that are having growing direct and indirect influence upon the fertility, mortality and migrations of their own populations as well as the populations of other countries, it is apparent that any speculation about the future of populations must include consideration of the uncertain political dimension as well as the more frequently considered social and economic dimensions.

Populations and Scale
Large and small countries differ demographically. Large countries contain much more internal diversity of populations, while small countries tend to be more volatile demographically – more affected by external migration

and more rapidly affected by changes in fertility and mortality – and also tend to have more irregular age–sex structures. When studying population phenomena and changes one must be aware of the effects of the scale of analysis. As far as we know, the world population has not so far been altered by immigration or emigration, only by natural change, the difference between births and deaths, so world projections only take them into account. On the other hand, among small populations the frequency of births and deaths is often less than that of external migration, which becomes the main cause of population change. In general, smaller units of population are affected more by net migration than by natural change. Hence, local and regional projections are mainly concerned with assumptions about migration. Micro- and macro-populations are therefore not immediately comparable, and so there is a danger in generalizing from local experience.

Similarly, the explanations of population phenomena alter with the scale of analysis. The factors influencing small populations may be quite different from those influencing large ones, sometimes invalidating international comparisons. For example, climate has a much greater role in influencing continental population distribution than local distribution, while housing quality is much more a determinant of local migration than of intercontinental migration. Consequently, there is little to be gained by comparing the population distribution and dynamics of countries which contrast dramatically in size like Singapore and China, or the Vatican City and Italy. The same is true for comparisons of different levels of internal subdivisions of states; comparing the population of a parish with that of a region is not comparing like with like.

Population Dynamics Yesterday and Today

Demographic Transition and Diversity

Demographic transition from high to low fertility and mortality has become a global social phenomenon comparable with the diffusion of the global economy, but variations in the way that it has affected populations around the world during the last two centuries have meant that they are now at very different stages in the process. Over a prolonged period during the nineteenth and early twentieth centuries, the more developed countries of Europe, North America and Oceania proceeded more or less gradually from high to low fertility and mortality. They did so at different times and rates, with intervening periods of more or less rapid population growth. The main engine was the decline in infant and child mortality, the various causes for which have been the subject of debate, followed by a reduction in fertility associated with a decline in the need for children, a rise in their cost and an emphasis on their quality. After the Second World War the developed countries were joined by Japan and all converged to growth rates well below 1 per cent per annum, sometimes even to negative rates, as seen in at least ten East European countries in recent years. Russia's current death rate of 16 per thousand is well in excess of its low birth rate of 9 per thousand, leading to an abnormal natural decrease rate of about 7 per thousand. Some developed countries are now in what may be called a post-transition phase, and will play a receding part in world population growth.

It is now accepted that this demographic transition was achieved by a wide combination of factors operating to a greater or lesser extent at different times and among different populations: improved social and cultural organization; advances in hygiene, sanitation, family planning and medical services, better nutrition and education; increased employment of women; as well as many other socio-economic changes associated with a shift from agricultural and mainly subsistence societies to urbanized, industrial and commercial societies. The transition was accompanied by the decline of the extended family, the rise of the small nuclear family and the reversal of intergenerational flows of wealth from upwards (children to parents) to downwards (parents to children).

Demographic transition in the more developed countries led to a remarkable ageing of population, whereby the young (aged under fifteen) declined from 40–50 per cent of the total population to less than 20 per cent. This resulted largely from a fall in average family size from over five children to well below two. In recent years, total fertility rates (TFRs, or the number of children a woman would have during the course of her life if she experienced the average fertility of the period at each age) have fallen as unexpectedly low as 1.2 to 1.3 children per woman in southern European countries such as Portugal, Spain, Italy and Greece. At the same time, in the more developed countries the percentage of the elderly aged sixty-five and over rose from less than 5 to more than 15, and in Sweden today the numbers of young and elderly are roughly equal at 18 per cent. With average longevity rising towards eighty years, the numbers of very old people aged eighty-five and over are increasing rapidly – in England and Wales they rose remarkably from 44,000 in 1901 to 948,000 in 1995. Unfortunately, most East European countries have not matched this progress in life expectancy, and some saw male life expectancy actually decline during the 1970s and 1980s. So far, the highest life expectancies have been achieved by

Japan: 76.6 for men and 83.0 for women. Generally there is a wide and growing gap between male and female longevity, so most developed countries have an increasing preponderance of elderly women, many of whom are widowed and living alone. The social and psychological problems of their isolation and vulnerability are rising rapidly.

In striking contrast, by the middle of the twentieth century most of the less developed countries were still characterized by high fertility, high but lowering mortality and burgeoning growth. Thus the dichotomy of more and less developed countries was then very clear from a demographic point of view. The high fertility of the less developed countries at that time meant that there would be great potential for population growth, even if fertility subsequently declined. In fact, they have experienced widely differing rates of decline in both mortality and fertility, mortality decline usually preceding that of fertility. The result has been diverse growth rates that today range from about 1 per cent to more than 3 per cent per annum, though even higher rates have been known. Consequently, the demographic contrast between the two groups of countries has been greatly attenuated, and some less developed countries (for example, China, South Korea) have experienced such kaleidoscoped demographic transition that they now have fertility and mortality rates not very dissimilar from those of the devleloped world. It has also rather dramatically decelerated the rate of world population growth from about 2.1 per cent per annum in the early 1970s to about 1.5 today.

Demographic transition in the less developed countries has generally been much faster than previously occurred in the more developed countries, especially as it was from higher pre-transition levels of fertility and mortality and among populations with universal and earlier marriage. It has taken place as a result of many factors including the diffusion of more effective contraception and improvements in the socio-economic status and education of women, along with better medical and health care leading to considerable reductions in infant and child mortality. Governments and international agencies have played a greater role in promoting demographic transition, supported by all branches of the media, which are having an increasing impact. Unfortunately, these demographic changes have not often been accompanied by the sort of social and economic developments that had been enjoyed by the advancing industrialized economies; they have occurred among populations living at much lower average income levels. When mortality declines and fertility does not, governments are faced with acute problems of rising numbers to educate, feed and employ.

The changes have been so very uneven that the less developed world is no longer universally characterized by high population growth rates. Certainly, relatively high fertility and mortality and persistently rapid population growth (about 3 per cent) still prevail in most of Sub-Saharan Africa, despite evidence of general mortality decline during the period 1950–90 and more recent fertility declines in some individual countries (for example, Kenya, Botswana, Zimbabwe, South Africa). Countries like Malawi, Mali and Niger have very youthful populations with high TFRs about 7, birth rates above 50 per thousand and relatively high but declining death rates approaching 20 per thousand. Unfortunately, the demography mirrors the low economic growth, unstable political conditions and widespread poverty within much of this region, and which are also common in parts of South Asia, as for example in Afghanistan and Burma.

In great contrast, substantially slower population growth (about 1 per cent) now occurs in much of populous East Asia and parts of South-East Asia, where both fertility and mortality have plummeted in recent decades among large populations in China, Taiwan, South Korea and Thailand as well as in smaller populations in Singapore, Hong Kong and Macao. Lesser transitions have taken place in many other countries, for example Indonesia and Sri Lanka, and in most Latin American countries. Accordingly, average life expectancies among less developed countries now range widely from about forty-five years in some African countries to over seventy-five in the newly industrializing countries of East Asia. While the former still have broadly based age–sex pyramids reflecting more decline in mortality than fertility, the latter are now experiencing rapid population ageing through fewer children and larger numbers of younger and middle adults.

In between these two poles, there are numerous developing countries with intermediate and declining birth rates (say 20–30 per thousand) and low or very low death rates below 10 per thousand and sometimes, where populations are still very young, even as low as 5 per thousand, as in some Pacific and Caribbean island states. India finds itself in this intermediate situation; between 1970 and 1992 its TFR dropped from 5.3 to 3.6, but its rate of population growth is still as high as 1.9.

So although there is a good case for considering the global population as an entity, responsive to global social, economic and political forces, the demographies of state populations have never been more diverse. As in the economic sphere, there is now a demographic spectrum, with certain regions changing much more rapidly than others, rather than a clear North–South divide, a term which is gradually losing its meaning.

Marked Inequalities
Growing demographic diversity has been accompanied by growing human inequality. Calculating human develop-

ment by life expectancy, education (as measured by adult literacy and school enrolment rates) and standard of living (as measured by gross domestic product), the United Nations *Human Development Report 1996* shows that the spectrum in human and economic development is widening all the time. Over the period 1980–95, the dramatic economic growth in fifteen countries (including the booming economies of Asia such as China, the Republic of Korea and Malaysia) containing 1.5 billion people, or about a quarter of the world's total, contrasted strongly with the worsening economies of about 100 countries incorporating a slightly larger number of people. Even more striking, it estimated that the assets of the world's 358 billionaires obscenely exceed the combined annual incomes of countries accounting for 45 per cent of the world's population. While the richest are inundated with consumer goods, the World Health Organization has estimated that about 1.1 billion people are living in extreme poverty, the underlying cause of short life expectancy, high maternal, infant and child mortality, malnutrition, disability and many other sufferings.

Within countries, social inequality is also strong and growing, and is reflected in wide variations in illness, disease, death and crime, as well as in many other ways. Although the links between wealth, health and death are not rigid, even in Britain death rates at all ages are two to three times higher among the most disadvantaged groups than among the most affluent groups, and they die about eight years earlier. Among the fifty states of the United States, those with the lowest income differentials have the lowest crude death rates, and the lowest rates for most of the main causes of death. Developed countries with the longest life expectancies tend to be those which are the most egalitarian, such as Japan and Sweden, with higher levels of investment in human development; and the same has proved true in less developed countries, good examples being China, Cuba and Sri Lanka.

Recent decades have revealed that there is no automatic link between the amount of economic growth and progress in human development. The structure and quality of economic growth play a vital role in human development. To be effective in human development, economic growth should expand employment opportunities, reduce poverty and inequality, improve human rights (including women's reproductive rights), increase democracy, avoid environmental degradation and enhance investment in education, health and the skills of people. Although such goals are well recognized, we are a long way from achieving them, and the currently growing disparities between and within countries should be a cause for great concern. They will certainly continue to be a prime reason for migrations, both international and internal.

Population Redistribution and Concentration

Growing international inequalities in birth, life and death have had a major impact on the uneven continental balance of population distribution. Despite overseas migrations during the nineteenth century by tens of millions of Europeans and lesser numbers of Asians, and the enormous impact that they had upon the Americas, Africa and Oceania, the populations of Europe and Asia continued to account for over 85 per cent of the world population during most of that century. In contrast, the percentage of Africans oscillated between 7 and 10, and the rising combined total population of the Americas and Oceania represented even less than this.

The twentieth century, especially the second half, has seen not only much greater world population growth, but the increasing preponderance of Asians. Since mid-century they have risen from 55 to 59 per cent of the world total, but there have been even more rapid rises in the relative numbers of Africans and Latin Americans to nearly 14 and 9 per cent respectively. In strong contrast, the percentage of Europeans has more than halved during the twentieth century, from 27 to 13, while that of North Americans declined slightly from just above 5 to just below, as flows of transoceanic migrants dwindled.

Intercontinental migrations have been massively out-numbered by the waves of other migrations which have helped to transform the overall distribution of humanity over the last two centuries. At the beginning of the nine-teenth century, as now, there were vast areas of the earth's surface uninhabited or very sparsely inhabited, usually because of hostile environmental conditions caused by hyper-aridity, high altitude and harsh cold, but the more favoured inhabited areas, sometimes called the ecumene, were much more evenly peopled than now. At that time only about 3 per cent of the billion inhabitants lived in towns; all the rest were in rural areas, in villages, hamlets and isolated dwellings, living largely from agriculture. The most populous regions coincided with the prolonged peas-ant civilizations of China, India and Europe, rather than with the location of natural resources, many of which were awaiting discovery and exploitation by later industrial and agricultural development.

The industrial and agricultural revolutions were the initial trigger of huge increases in human mobility, facili-tated by technical developments in transport by sea, rail, road and air. They precipitated massive international and internal migrations, the latter less inhibited by boundaries than the former. Above all, millions moved from the countryside to the towns, many of which emerged in the first place as industrial centres on or near to sources of power and raw materials, especially the great coalfields, or as city-ports acting as gateways for growing international trade. This process of urbanization and population concentration subsequently diffused (along with numerous other phenomena) from Europe to the 'New Europes' overseas, and to many other parts of the world, linking them with the world economy and contributing to the increasing concentration of populations and cities around the coastal fringes of the continents, contrasting with relatively low densities in the interiors.

Urbanization, which began with the growth of industry and commerce, has been accelerated during the twentieth century not only by revolutionary changes in the primary and secondary sectors of economies, but also by an enormous growth in all aspects of the service sector in all countries, particularly in the developing world. As a result, global urbanization has been much more rapid than global population growth. By the mid-1990s about 45 per cent of the world's population were living in towns, and the proportion is growing continually. It is difficult to be really precise because definitions of 'urban' vary so much from country to country, based on classification of settlements according to their administrative status, population size and/or economic activities.

Affecting all inhabited areas of the world, urbanization is now most rapid in those parts of the world with fastest population growth, the less developed countries. There, mega-cities with many millions of inhabitants are increasingly dominating their urban hierarchies, as we see in Brazil, Egypt, Mexico and Thailand, provoking strong rural–urban disequilibrium. Many capital cities of newly independent states have grown mercurially, particularly in very centralized unitary states; in more devolved federal states they tend to be less dominant. Some of the urban giants of the developing world, like Mexico City, São Paulo, Shanghai, Seoul and Bombay, are overtaking in size the largest cities of the developed world, although as yet most have not achieved the 'world city' status of London, New York and Tokyo, which are 'cotter pins' of the present world economy. Size isn't everything.

In contrast, many larger cities of developed countries such as the United Kingdom have experienced a reversal of the trend towards population growth. Sometimes known as counter-urbanization or urban deconcentration, and facilitated by massive changes in transport, it is causing many cities to diminish in population or spread out. Unlike the less developed countries, the population distributions of these developed countries are also achieving a measure of dynamic equilibrium, in which high levels of mobility produce low net migration and relatively little change in overall population distribution. Short-term circulation is much more common than long-term migration. One result of these contrasting processes of population redistribution is that the population maps of countries like the United Kingdom or France change much less than those of Nigeria or Venezuela.

Viewed globally, urbanization has provoked pronounced population concentration, especially because larger cities tend to be localized within the rather restricted economic core areas of countries which also tend to be coastal in location. Generally these core areas contain ever higher proportions of countries' populations, at the expense of the more marginal areas, many of which, in rich and poor countries alike, suffer from the malaise of rural depopulation. It has been estimated recently that nearly two-thirds of the world's population live within 60 kilometres of the coast, where some huge populations of coastal lowlands and deltas, notably in Asia and Africa, fear the possibility of rising sea levels resulting from the 'greenhouse effect', one aspect of global environmental change.

Population Dynamics Tomorrow

World Fertility Decline

The future of fertility is the key speculation in population projections, because usually it exceeds mortality and is now the main determinant of population growth. Unlike mortality, fertility is neither individual nor inevitable nor involuntary. Fertility is less constant and predictable than mortality, and it tends to fluctuate in response to many social, economic and political factors. Unlike deaths, which may occur at any age, births occur only to women in the reproductive age-groups (mostly within a fairly narrow age-band, although this is changing), and they are more preventable. Births also have a longer-term impact upon populations than deaths, through their effects on the numbers of future generations.

Children survive much more than in the past and are less of an economic asset, so more and more people are anxious to curb their reproduction. Moreover, the rapid world population growth of recent decades has encouraged enormous efforts to lower fertility by numerous governments as well as international and national non-governmental organizations. Few countries have not experienced some fertility decline. This 'reproductive revolution' has become part of the global belief system, affecting not only the developing world but also the West, from which it originated. Consequently, the world TFR has slumped from around 5 at mid-century to about 3 today, and the overall TFR of less developed countries has dropped from 6 to 3.1. We should expect this decline to continue. It will certainly not be consistent or uniform, but the direction is sure, and it will have profound effects upon most populations of the world.

Nearly all the more developed countries have already achieved levels of fertility generally well below replacement, exceptions being Malta and Iceland, and it is difficult to imagine these levels rising markedly. It is feasible that the current very low TFRs prevailing in some Mediterranean countries may be associated with specific social changes and may not persist for very long. Similarly, the turmoil arising from the passing of socialism may account for the low fertility in many East European countries and that may be short-lived. As Sweden has already demonstrated, babies can come back into fashion; tax changes favouring a second child and delayed child-bearing, a common phenomenon now in European countries experiencing rising female employment, have helped in the last few years to restore fertility rates to near replacement levels. But this may be just a temporary upturn. The main likelihood is that many advanced countries face a future of fluctuating low levels of fertility. All the present social and economic trends point in that direction: the decline of marriage and the family; the growing frequency of cohabitation and divorce; the increasing status, education and employment of women; and the ever-rising material aspirations and demands of consumer-orientated societies. Although these trends vary in level and pace from country to country, and are generally further advanced in North America, Oceania and Western Europe than in Southern and Eastern Europe, there is no reason to expect a U-turn in any of these social processes. Oscillations, yes; reversals, unlikely.

Scope for further fertility decline in all of these more developed countries lies in still numerous unplanned pregnancies, especially among teenagers. In the United States, it is estimated that there are about a million teenage pregnancies each year, four-fifths of them unintentional, and that 57 per cent of all pregnancies are unintended. Clearly there is an 'unmet need' for family planning, which will be met in the future. In Britain, which has the highest number of teenage pregnancies in Europe, the National Health Service is particularly concerned with this multifaceted problem, which has led to high abortion rates among adolescents, and it is targeting teenagers through its outreach services. But Britain lacks the sort of effective sex education in primary and junior schools that is given in the Netherlands, where teenage pregnancies have been greatly reduced. In general, the nature of family planning services and prevailing attitudes to sex influence their uptake and fertility. Improvements in contraceptive methods and practice may be delayed temporarily by a litigious marketplace, but in the long run surely they will reduce unplanned pregnancies to the advantage of all. Couples will still wish to have one or two children, so although replacement levels of 2.1 children may not be achieved, except perhaps in North America, we should not expect fertility levels to go below 1.0, even in West European countries where they are currently very low.

One of the more difficult tasks is to predict the percentage of children born to unmarried parents. In Britain it has risen from 6 per cent in 1960 to about one-third today, three-quarters of them being born to consensual unions and the rest to single parents. This dramatic social trend, repeated to a greater or lesser extent in most developed countries, but not in Japan, is dissociating fertility from marriage. We may have to wait several generations to see the full social effects, especially upon the education of children, but the trend shows no sign of abating as more and more women are taking up careers and are unwilling to be constrained by the traditional ties of marriage and the family. Obviously, there may well be a reaction to these processes, but again it may take several decades.

The real problem of predicting fertility lies among the less developed countries, where there is so much diversity in fertility levels, educational attainments, reproductive health and availability of contraception. Nearly all these countries have undergone some fertility decline during recent decades, but the large-scale World Fertility Survey during 1972–86 and the subsequent national Demographic and Health Surveys conducted since 1986 have revealed that women's actual fertility is up to two children above their desired fertility, and that there is a huge range (about 5 to 70 per cent) in the proportion of women aged fifteen to forty-four using contraception. So the overall unmet need is enormous. From surveys, it is estimated that in less developed countries there are over 100 million women married or in union who have an unmet need for limiting or spacing births, nearly a third of them in India. They are also especially numerous in Pakistan, Bangladesh, Nigeria, Indonesia, Brazil and Mexico, but still substantial even in Asian countries like Thailand and Sri Lanka which have already achieved considerable fertility decline. It is also true that in most countries husbands want more children than their wives, so family planners are now focusing attention on men.

About 15 million women aged under twenty give birth each year, accounting for one-fifth of all births, and most are in less developed countries. Moreover, an average delay of a year between starting sexual activity and the first use of contraception means that there is a huge number of unintended pregnancies among teenagers, the avoidance of which must surely be a primary goal. Contraception freely available to all is a daunting target, but better family planning services and communications will go a long way, especially if combined with cheaper contraceptives and greater contraceptive expenditure. At the moment, it is only a tiny fraction of the expenditure on arms and conflicts.

Fertility decline is not just a matter of planning and money. Nor are programmes in fertility reduction the prerogative of authoritarian regimes, such as in China. Despite the cultural context of fertility, growing awareness of population issues worldwide has made fertility decline a major social phenomenon of our time. Even in fundamentalist Iran, the TFR has almost halved since the Islamic revolution of 1979. The main question is the rate of future fertility decline. In the near future it will probably advance most where it has advanced most already, but with ever improving communications we should expect the laggards to follow the leaders, even if most East and West African countries, where fertility is highest, take several decades longer to effect the fertility transition. The poorest countries will not always have the highest fertility, and in the long run there will be an evening out of fertility differentials.

The Future for Women
Critical to the future of fertility decline is the future for women. Although advantaged demographically by their greater longevity and biological resilience, in many other ways women have been more disadvantaged than men in most societies: by inferior education, lower literacy, earlier marriage, excessive child-bearing, son and male preference, prolonged widowhood, fewer economic opportunities and limited political power. These features were usually sustained by their incorporation into the major cultural systems. Only with the rise and widespread diffusion of Western industrial and commercial urbanized societies and their accompanying demographic and social changes, including increasing individualism, have we witnessed remarkable changes in women's roles and status.

In general, those changes have been greatest in the more developed and newly industrializing countries, and least where agricultural societies and/or religious fundamentalisms prevail. Now the international variations in female roles and status are so immense that it is one of the most diverse aspects of demographic structures, greatly affecting fertility, mortality and migration. This is despite the difficulty in defining female status from a demographic viewpoint; marked improvements in demographic variables, such as women's rising age at marriage, reduced child-bearing and higher levels of literacy and labour-force participation, may not always be accompanied by differences in their psychological status, as in the case of many Japanese women.

Many studies have shown that improvements in female education have been of key importance in lowering fertility, by delaying marriage and the onset of child-bearing, increasing female employment, raising female status, reducing desired family size and enabling women to use contraception more effectively. The gap between the fertility of educated and of uneducated women is generally growing in the less developed countries, is widest when fertility declines most rapidly, and is much more significant than the fertility difference between rich and poor women. Education and social advance of women in the less developed countries are therefore regarded as more important in reducing fertility than a rise in their economic status, although when they occur in combination they produce powerful changes in marriage patterns and family size, as can be seen in many East Asian countries today. But even in low-fertility societies women will still face major challenges in balancing multiple activities.

We are looking forward to a continued rise in female status in many developing countries. The demand for it clearly dominated the 1994 International Conference on Population and Development in Cairo, and it is becoming an irresistible tidal wave which will affect most parts of the world. Disseminated by the media, it is becoming another part of the global belief system. Of course, there is some cultural and political resistance, but even in those countries experiencing little modernization or a resurgence of religious fundamentalism its progress will be only partially restrained.

Declining Mortality and Increasing Ageing

Future mortality is generally more predictable than future fertility, because death is inevitable and is greatly influenced by existing age structures. Indeed, mortality is usually expressed by life expectancy at birth, which is a summary of age-specific mortality rates at a particular time (that is, rates calculated to express the incidence of deaths within age-groups).

Most populations in the world have experienced mortality decline in recent decades, but how much more decline can we expect? Considerable further reductions can be made, but we should remind ourselves that mortality decline is a complex phenomenon, its various determinants acting in combination rather than in isolation. Obviously, its progress differs around the world.

In the most advanced countries, life expectancies are generally higher now than ever previously imagined, soaring well above the traditional 'three score years and ten', a life-span which generally they achieved more than three decades ago. Life expectancies are rising by about two years a decade, and we may confidently expect this progress to continue. Death rates among older age groups over seventy-five and eighty-five are declining so rapidly in many advanced countries that definitions of old age are being intermittently adjusted upwards; sixty and sixty-five are no longer regarded as old, though people are usually retiring earlier. Unfortunately, increasing longevity has not been accompanied by more years of healthy life; in Britain a sixty-five-year-old can still look forward to only seven years of healthy life. Healthier lifestyles would have a major impact, and increasing efforts are being made in health promotion. Reduction in socio-economic and ethnic inequalities would also bring about further improvements in mortality, even without any dramatic medical progress in curing the current main killer diseases: cancers, ischaemic heart disease and cerebrovascular disease. Recent evidence does not point to any marked reduction, but surely the persistence of sharp inequalities would provoke severe political and social reaction, so in the long run we should hope for and expect more egalitarian societies with more equal mortality rates.

A key question about further mortality decline in developed countries is how long people can survive. Ageing is a natural process, and eventually high and rising life expectancies are bound to level off. At present, there is considerable debate about the maximum biological age and what proportion of a population might achieve it. Until recently, some put this maximum at 120 with average life expectancies rising to about 85, but now 130 years seems more likely with average life expectancies in the twenty-first century continuing to climb towards 90, as numbers dying earlier would diminish. The lack of a major world war for half a century has reduced the mortality of younger adults, and medical progress has permitted many unhealthy people to survive longer, but perhaps not to an average age. On balance, we should not expect a great leap forward in mortality decline, merely steady progress.

Certainly, there will continue to be a marked rise in the numbers of those aged eighty-five and over, sometimes called the 'oldest old'. Projections suggest that in England and Wales they will increase by three-quarters by 2025. Then, as in most countries of North and West Europe, about one-tenth of the population will be aged seventy-five and over and between a quarter and a third aged sixty and over. The numbers of centenarians will grow even more rapidly; data for fourteen developed countries during the 1980s showed their extraordinary increase rate of 8–10 per cent a year, with more than four times as many women as men. One recent estimate suggests that in England and Wales they will increase tenfold by 2031 to exceed 45,000.

As for those more conventionally regarded as the old populations, those aged sixty-five and over, projections show that by the 2020s they will constitute higher but variable proportions of total populations of developed countries. While in Britain and the United States they will comprise about 16–17 per cent, in France and Italy they will be nearer 20 per cent, in Germany 22 per cent and in Japan about 24 per cent. Much depends upon the inescapable demographic past of countries. Thus Japan's high fertility before the Second World War, its post-war 'baby boom' (when the TFR was about 4.5), the subsequent striking fertility decline following its 1948 Law of Eugenics Protection, and its rapid reduction in mortality all help to account for its future rise to the dubious distinction of having the oldest population among the major powers. In contrast, Britain's much lower fertility before the late 1940s and its difficulty in lowering mortality mean much slower ageing in the next century.

Whatever the precise levels and rates of ageing, all developed countries will have to adjust to more rectangular population structures as the twenty-first century progresses. Older populations in their 'third age' will require more and different health care and more appropriate retail and leisure services. The elderly will engage even more in the vast voluntary sector, and their vacations will be orientated increasingly toward centres of history and culture, especially in warmer climes. Their attitudes to crime, law and order will influence governments, and older members of electorates will have greater political power. One particular problem is how societies will treat their rapidly growing numbers of very old people – by integrating them into their communities or by segregating them in residential and nursing homes? Despite the mushrooming numbers of homes and the increasing breakdown of families, sustained integration is generally preferred by the elderly themselves.

All this is far removed from future patterns of mortality and ageing in less developed countries. Their considerable progress in mortality decline during the second half of the twentieth century – when average life expectancy rose from about forty years to nearly sixty-five – was very uneven, and that will unfortunately persist for the foreseeable future. The profound mortality declines in much of Asia, notably East Asia, and in Latin America and the Caribbean, may be expected to continue, as many countries have demonstrated that economic growth is not essential to mortality decline. Countries in these regions will experience ageing populations to a greater or lesser extent, none more so than China, whose rapid demographic transition in recent decades ensures that its elderly population will grow mercurially in the next century: by the 2020s it is expected that the sixty-plus-year-olds will increase from 10 to 20 per cent.

In unfortunate contrast, mortality decline is likely to be much more limited in Sub-Saharan Africa, which in recent decades has suffered numerous catastrophes, natural and man-made. Economic difficulties, failing health services, malnutrition, epidemics, poverty and political problems have meant that there has been little progress in the 'epidemiological transition', whereby infectious diseases are replaced by those of ageing as the main cause of death. Indeed, in many countries deaths from infectious diseases such as malaria, tuberculosis, dengue fever and sexually transmitted diseases are rising. Most striking has been the recent but devastating impact of the AIDS pandemic. Mainly a heterosexual disease in Africa disseminated by multiple relationships, it currently affects about seventeen countries, adding substantially to overall mortality rates. In parts of East Africa it reduces catastrophically the agricultural workforce and creates innumerable orphans. Unfortunately, its full effects are yet to be seen, and will last for generations, so it is a big question mark for the future. Of course Africa is not alone; the disease is diffusing rapidly in Asian countries, especially in Thailand, where the sex industry is notorious, as well as in Latin America. It has been estimated by John Bongaarts that the number in the world infected with HIV will rise from 18.5 million in mid-1995, over half of them in Sub-Saharan Africa, to 47.4 million in 2005, when Asian numbers will approach those of Africa.

The fact that most Sub-Saharan African populations have undergone less demographic transition than other regions of the less developed world – Mauritius, Réunion and South Africa are notable exceptions – means that they will experience much less ageing in future decades. They will not be entirely spared, but they will remain the youngest (and the poorest) populations in the world, the average age remaining in the low twenties at least until 2030 – about half what it will be in Western Europe. In the West, we have our concerns in adjusting to ageing populations, but Africa has much more serious concerns in tackling poverty and population growth in a continent wracked also with severe political and environmental problems.

Future Mobility and Migrations
Of the three components of population change, migration is the most difficult to predict. Unlike fertility and mortal-

ity, migration takes place in both time and space, and may be renewed or reversed. Migrations also vary greatly in cause, course, duration, distance, volume, selectivity and organization, and they have very different impacts upon population patterns. The European settlements of the New World transformed the population map, whereas the innumerable internal movements in industrialized countries do little more than consolidate existing patterns. Generally, migration movements are more intermittent, spasmodic and fluctuating than either fertility or mortality, especially when the causes are mainly political or environmental, as after the fall of the Berlin Wall or during Sahel droughts. Past migration flows are therefore not a reliable guide to future flows, so trend analysis is not very helpful. Perhaps not surprisingly, demographers have generally given less attention to migrations than to other components of population change, and there has been no sufficiently robust migration transition theory to be as widely accepted as demographic transition theory for use in making population projections. Yet among the populations of the more developed countries, which are neither growing nor declining very much, migration is the key component of internal population change and sometimes externally as well. It will require much more attention in the future.

A further complication is that the migration component of overall population change is net migration, the balance between opposing independent emigration and immigration flows (or between out-migration and in-migration flows within a country), which may not reflect the volumes of those flows at all. For instance, two powerful opposing migration streams, one of which may be return migration, may result in little or no net migration. In addition, the accuracy of migration projections is not helped by the paucity and inadequacy of statistics, particularly when disasters provoke flights of refugees or when illegal/clandestine migration is important. No wonder that considerations about future migrations tend to be highly speculative.

One point we can be sure about is that human mobility, that is the displacement of individuals, will continue to increase, and that it will be less and less constrained by distance. An example of the accelerating collapse of long-distance space is that, while the population of Australia has doubled since the Second World War, annual movements in and out have multiplied a hundred times, despite its remoteness from other countries. Although there has been a mercurial surge in instant communications by telephone, facsimile, E-mail and the World Wide Web, there is little evidence to suggest that in the short run it will reduce overall distances travelled or human mobility. On the other hand, it is greatly multiplying exchanges, enabling firms to find cheaper locations, 'urban refugees' to become 'telecommuters' and more people to work from home. Thus it reduces the isolation of rural communities and the separateness of regions; and advances the inexorable progress of globalization.

In many ways, mobility reflects the rapid change in societies. It is fuelled by factors such as the growth in population, inequalities and technologies, the reduction in ties to local resources, the huge growth in service industries, the frequent changes in the labour market and the increasing employment of women. Already women are becoming ever more numerous in all types of mobility and migration, and that will continue as their economic activities expand, though their movements will still be more influenced than those of men by their family roles.

The forms of mobility will become increasingly complex, particularly within countries, and the growth of transnational companies, trade and tourism will make the dichotomy between internal and international migrations even more artificial. There will be a particular increase in all types of short-term circulatory movements to work and leisure, which are repetitive and cyclical, and the difference between temporary and permanent movements will also become less and less clear. Not only will average transport costs get cheaper and average travel distances per person get longer, but increasing mobility will be constrained less by a specific place of residence and the distance from it.

All this poses particular problems for demographers, who have traditionally defined a migration somewhat ambiguously as a permanent or semi-permanent movement of persons crossing a certain boundary to establish a new residence. They have difficulty in statistically analysing the mobility of modern societies, where more and more people have multiple residences, workplaces and household incomes, and there are more and more long-distance commuters, migrant workers and retirees, students living away from home and long-term travellers. The locations of residence and workplace cannot be regarded as singular, stable and proximate; they are often dysfunctional with increasing aggregate travel to work. Even in developing countries many new city-dwellers regard themselves as multilocal, retaining close links with their former rural homes and returning there frequently and often permanently after retirement. Consequently, we should think less about the specific locations of people and more about their expanding living spaces.

Foreseeably, space travel will not alter the world's total population through net migration. It will be changed only by natural increase, and so its projections are simpler than at sub-global levels. At the lowest level, the populations of most streets will have more arrivals and departures than births and deaths, and probably more net migration than natural increase. At national level, most people stay in their home countries. In 1994 it was estimated (probably underestimated) that 125 million or 2.2 per cent of the world's population were living outside their home countries. That percentage may increase, but the part played by international migration in population change will generally be much less than that of natural change, except in countries where that is very low or in some small countries (for example, Gulf and Caribbean states) where either immigrants will outnumber nationals or emigrants will relieve population pressure. Nobody suggests that emigration and the remittances of migrants will solve major population pressures, like those of Bangladesh or Egypt. Their solutions must lie elsewhere. It has been suggested, however, that when rapidly increasing populations are unable to find safety valves in emigration, they turn more readily to family limitation, but that proposition is not easy to prove, because so many other factors are involved.

International migrations will be influenced by a host of other phenomena, such as economic and demographic differences, environmental conditions, cultural contrasts, political conflicts and government policies. In particular, the evolving geopolitical situation will have conflicting effects on international migration streams; while globalization will encourage them, growing nationalism will discourage them. Much will depend on future political systems and groupings. If the number of states continues to grow, we can expect a sharp increase in the number of international migrants. But boundaries will remain as barriers unless countered, perhaps unexpectedly, by changing attitudes to international inequalities and inequities. The rich world is showing less compassion to poorer international migrants, and yet 'we all come from somewhere else' and are all members of the same human family.

Most migration streams will continue to be up the economic ladder, a feature which is intensifying as it lengthens. They will not be orientated merely to the most developed countries. Newly industrializing and/or oil-rich countries, like the Gulf States, Malaysia, Venezuela and South Africa, have already joined the more developed countries as prime target destinations for migrants, and many of them will receive more, often from remote sources. Most migrants, however, will want to enter the wealthy West, but many countries, notably in the European Union, will be exercising stricter controls over the influx, despite their ageing populations. Finding themselves faced with high unemployment rates, deindustrialization, growing automation, increasing competition and problems of integrating their ethnic minorities, they are no longer so welcoming to migrant manual workers from non-European countries, especially when they may receive more skilled workers from other member states of the Union. Their new transnational space is becoming an exclusive club ever more closed to the poorer countries. The essentially migrant populations of the United States and Canada have stronger traditions of openness and assimiliation of foreigners, and, like Australia and New Zealand, have much lower population pressures which will ensure that they will continue to attract immigration streams from most parts of the world. But, as in Europe, the great problem of illegal/clandestine migrants will not go away.

Sadly, political instability and strife in many newly independent poorer countries will mean that tens of millions of their rapidly growing populations will become, as now, political refugees. Their numbers will be spasmodic and their locations uncertain, but as now they will be concentrated especially in Sub-Saharan Africa and parts of Asia, where many newly independent states offer little social, economic or political security to the individual, where human rights may be limited, where poverty prevails, where state conflicts are all too common, and where more and more people know from the media that things are better elsewhere. In some cases, it will be difficult to distinguish between political refugees and those who are fleeing from environmental disasters and are now sometimes (controversially) called environmental refugees. The causes of flight are often blurred. Few refugees will find refuge outside these regions, and they will continue to put enormous strains on the limited economies, fragile ecologies and delicate ethnic balances in some of the poorest and most troubled parts of the world. The recent fragmentation of the former federal states of the Soviet Union and Yugoslavia and the flights of refugees from Chechnya and Bosnia have also removed any complacency in Europe about refugees being no longer a European problem.

Regrettably, ethnic tensions and conflicts will ensure that there will always be political refugees, and growing environmental pressures and degradation combined with the certainty of catastrophes and disasters will guarantee that there will be environmental refugees. Consequently, a much greater international effort is necessary to deal with the problems of refugees as well as the conditions which cause refugee flows, because they intensify international inequalities which are already becoming increasingly unacceptable. But that will require a dramatic change in attitudes towards solving some of the root causes of refugee movements and of international migrations in general: the need in source countries for broader sustainable economic growth, greater investment, more democracy, better protection of human rights, and expanded access to family planning services.

Decelerating World Population Growth

World population growth is decelerating, and that is likely to continue. We shall not return to the high growth rate of the 1960s. Recent fertility decline means that the ultimate stationary population of the world may be nearer 12 billion than the much higher figures previously forecast. Without going into precise projections or looking too far into the future, we can be fairly confident that by the year 2030 the world's population will approach 8 billion, but that will arise from vastly different growth rates around the world. By then, nearly 7 million people will be living in countries which will have completed the demographic transition, including Asian, Latin American and North African countries as well as the present developed countries. We have little experience of the post-transition phase of the developed countries; we expect few major changes, but we cannot be sure. The one certainty is continued ageing.

Recent projections up to 2030 suggest that population growth in the more developed countries will be relatively slow, so as presently constituted their proportion of the world's population will decline quite dramatically from 22 per cent in 1990 to about 14 per cent. Growth during that period will be especially slow in Western Europe, where it will probably be only about 10 per cent, in comparison with a North American rate three to four times as high. Some European countries, including Britain, may see their populations plateau before then and begin to decline. The minority status of the rich countries will therefore be intensified. Already, most are less concerned with overall population growth than with numerous structural, ethical and distributional issues: caring for the very old; problems of pensions; fluctuating cohorts; growing ethnic minorities; artificial insemination and abortion; increasing cohabitation, divorce and one-parent families; numbers of unemployed; transport difficulties; availability of housing; and the provision of educational and health services. In short, although in relative terms these populations are relatively wealthy, they are and will be more concerned about their quality of life than with overall numbers of people.

In contrast, recent projections suggest that probably 95 per cent of world population growth until 2030 will take place in those countries currently termed less developed or developing, which will contain over 85 per cent of the world total. But there will be massive variations. While China's population is expected to grow by merely a half, roughly the world average, that of Latin America will probably grow by three-quarters, while the population of Southern Asia will more than double in size. Much more speculatively, that of Sub-Saharan Africa may nearly triple, despite the considerable uncertainty about the future impact of AIDS, malaria and many other phenomena. Thus by 2030 China's percentage of world population will decline from 22 to 18, while Africa's is expected to overtake China's by increasing from 12 to 19. In other words, the regional balance of world population distribution will change substantially, with the poorest regional populations generally growing the fastest to accentuate still more the world pattern of growing inequality. The persistence of poverty will delay substantially the stabilization of overall world population.

Future Population Patterns

Growing Concentration of Population

Largely because most future population growth will take place in the less developed countries, the world's population will become increasingly concentrated over the next few decades at least. This will occur in several different ways. First, by 2030 two of the three largest concentrations of humankind, those in East and South Asia (the other is in Europe), will together accumulate over 4.1 billion people, about 1.8 billion more than now. They will contain, as now, some 44 per cent of humanity on a little over 13 per cent of the world's land area. If we add in the rest of East and South-East Asia, we will find that nearly 54 per cent of the world's population will be living around the southern and eastern fringes of Asia.

Secondly, the inhabited areas of the earth will not be extended appreciably in the foreseeable future, nor will the world map of population distribution be radically changed. It reflects the long-term past rather than the optimum distribution of the present, but the political map will ensure that it largely retains its present patterns. Although the expansion of agricultural land through clearing, draining and irrigation will continue to bring pressure on the fringes, few of the vast uninhabited areas, which account for nearly seven-tenths of the land area, will witness the sort of frontier settlements common during the eighteenth and nineteenth centuries and that paved the way for the current world population map. Much of the non-ecumene will be exploited, and new urban centres will arise, but its environmental difficulties are generally too severe for large-scale dense human habitation. The sparsely inhabited interiors of the continents will not suddenly become attractive to intensive human occupation; many are far too remote from the global economy and too environmentally unattractive. Tropical rainforests are suffering from excessive clearings with damaging ecological results, but they are not attracting enough population redistribution to alter significantly the population map. No, for better or worse the existing ecumene will comprise nearly all the expected population growth. For example, the arid world already contains too many people – 15 per cent of the world's population on 37 per cent of its land area – but most are localized along the semi-arid fringes or well-watered valleys of less developed countries, such as the Nile, Tigris, Euphrates and Indus, which are thus predicted to become even more populated, and pose greater problems of water supply and environmental degradation.

Thirdly, within the inhabited areas of most countries there will be growing polarization of population distribution, as economic core areas, such as those in south-east Brazil and Java, will contain a growing proportion of populations. The exodus from marginal areas will persist, accelerated from time to time by environmental and human disasters, and as the migrants will largely comprise people within the reproductive age-groups the source areas will also experience further fertility decline. Of course, very many countries already have extremely skewed population distributions, notably nearly seventy with large desert or semi-desert sectors, like Egypt, Algeria, Australia and Chile. This will not change. The populous areas will just become more populous. Attempts by governments to reverse population polarization particularly in coastal zones have so far been largely ineffective, even when authoritarian governments, as in China, have had deliberate redistribution policies. Only in the more developed countries will we see a slowing down of rural depopulation, as population distributions become more stabilized. Even there, depopulation will tend to continue from remote and more difficult areas, but those peri-urban areas within ready access to urban centres will see further population pressure from long-distance commuters and suburban expansion, and further pressure on land for amenities (for example, golf courses, airports).

Fourthly, rapid urban population growth will continue apace in less developed countries. We must expect that the rate of urban population growth will exceed that of rural population growth through a combination of in-migration, natural increase and the incorporation of surrounding villages into expanding cities. Naturally, the rate of urban population growth will vary appreciably across the Third World, but it will be fastest in those regions which were previously feebly urbanized and where population growth is currently most rapid, as for example in East Africa. By the year 2000, we can be sure that at least 45 per cent of more than 5 billion inhabitants of less developed countries will be living in urban areas, but by 2025 those countries will probably contain over 80 per cent of more than 5 billion urban dwellers in the world. This will mean that the urban populations of the Third World will have multiplied about fourteen times during the seventy-five years 1950–2025 – a massive metamorphosis which will be mainly resistant to policies to slow it down. Yet many poor countries will be quite unable to cope with such a change within their existing economies and administrative structures. Surprisingly, the prospect of this incredible population redistribution and the manifold problems associated with it have attracted far less attention than that of population growth *per se*.

The problem will be intensified because much of this

urbanization will be localized in burgeoning mega-cities, whose unprecedented absolute growth will far outstrip that of smaller towns and cause immense spatial concentration of population. By 2000, the number of cities with more than 4 million inhabitants in less developed countries is predicted to increase to forty-nine, including seventeen of the twenty largest cities in the world; five of them will be mega-cities with more than 15 million inhabitants, compared with only two in the more developed world. It has been projected that by 2025 about 28 per cent of the population of less developed countries will be living in large cities, roughly double the percentage for the more developed countries. The condition of these cities will vary greatly, but the implications for the provision of housing, infrastructure, employment, education, health and social services are monumental, as is the impact upon the physical environment, particularly because large city growth is happening so rapidly.

Concern about Carrying Capacity

Malthusian concern over the dramatic growth of world population during the twentieth century caused many, quite wrongly, to blame it excessively for most of the ills of humankind. It also revived considerable interest in 'carrying capacity', a biological concept which generally has much more validity with animals than with people. Human populations are greatly affected by their progressive technologies, reduced dependence upon local resources, and by the continuous process of globalization which interlinks economies and societies worldwide. The full force of globalization has yet to be felt. Modern societies will be less and less closed, more and more affected by international decisions. Consequently the population pressure on a relatively small area, say Singapore, County Durham or Ibiza, cannot be viewed in isolation, except, quite validly, in specific terms of environmental impact. When considering sustainability, a fashionable term that is not easily quantified, some have been more concerned about environmental degradation of a territory than the human development of a population, yet they are obviously interdependent.

Many, especially those with a pessimistic view about the future, have given thought to how many people the earth as a whole can support. Much depends on expectations and aspirations of future standards of living, which vary enormously around the world, and whether concerns are primarily human or environmental. Not surprisingly, the estimates, which are mostly by Westerners, range so widely, from 0.5 billion to 1,000 billion people, that they defy credibility. The rough current consensus is about 7.7 billion, a total that will be attained during the 2010s, but, given the continued deceleration in world population growth during the twenty-first century, it will not be so greatly exceeded as previously thought. The main problem is its uneven global distribution of population and its inequalities.

The Global Challenge of Inequalities

Despite increasing global concerns, population pressures have been tackled only at national and local level, where populations experience such diverse conditions. Over the last few decades, reducing the rate of population growth has been generally accepted as desirable by most countries. Fertility decline has become the key element in the population policies of high-fertility countries, and that will have increasingly beneficial effects in helping to reduce demographic diversity, as well as widespread poverty, population dependency burdens, the disempowerment of women and environmental degradation.

Fertility decline is not enough. It must also be matched

by economic growth in the poorer parts of the world, because the enormous economic disparities and inequities affecting so many of humankind cannot be justified. For example, according to ILO, nearly 1 billion people, about 30 per cent of the global workforce, are unemployed or under-employed, because of reduction of jobs in more developed countries and continuing crises in less developed countries. The reduction of economic inequalities through equitable and sustainable development of countries and their populations is a huge challenge facing humanity.

It must also be matched by human development, incorporating access not only to education, especially for women, a reduction in infant, child and maternal mortality, and improved living conditions for all, but also human rights and reproductive health. In the past, it has been assumed that individual welfare would benefit from collective population policies, but the demographic actions of many communist and authoritarian regimes have shown that this is clearly not true. Population policies have been too nationalistic, too exclusively demographic and insufficiently compatible with other policies. As governments become more interventionist, there is a major problem in reconciling individual rights with the collective good, especially of the global population. Population policies must be for people as well as for populations, and people should play a greater role in formulating them, particularly at local level. Policies must also display a fundamental commitment to ethics and human rights, and be concerned with quality of life (however difficult that is to define) as well as with the ecology of our earth. These transnational issues will not be solved by national governments alone, and will become ever more important in the twenty-first century as medical and scientific technologies have an even greater influence on human reproduction, movement and survival.

Acknowledgements

This short essay inevitably synthesizes a vast literature. Detailed references would have doubled its length and reduced its readability. Most of the material may be found in expanded form in volumes cited in Further Reading. I am particularly grateful to my daughter Lucy for her thoughts and ideas.

Further Reading

Cohen, Joel E., *How Many People Can the Earth Support?* (W. W. Norton, New York, 1995).

Colombo, Bernard, Demeny, Paul, and Perutz, Max F., (eds), *Resources and Population: Natural, Institutional, and Demographic Dimensions of Development* (Clarendon Press, Oxford, 1996).

Demeny, Paul and McNicoll, Geoffrey (eds), *The Earthscan Reader in Population and Development* (Earthscan, London, 1997).

Douglas, Ian, Huggett, Richard and Robinson, Mike (eds), *Companion Encyclopedia of Geography: The Environment and Humankind* (Routledge, London and New York, 1996).

Graham-Smith, Francis (ed.) *Population: The Complex Reality* (The Royal Society, London, 1994).

Kritz, Mary M., Lim, Lin Lean and Zlotnik, Hana (eds), *International Migration Systems: A Global Approach* (Clarendon Press, Oxford, 1992).

Lassonde, Louise, *Coping with Population Challenges* (Earthscan, London, 1996).

Livi-Bacci, Massimo, *A Concise History of World Population* (Blackwell, Oxford, 1992; 2nd edn 1997).

Lutz, Wolfgang, (ed.) *The Future Population of the World: What Can We Assume Today?* (Earthscan, London, 1994).

McRae, Hamish, *The World in 2020: Power, Culture and Prosperity: A Vision of the Future* (HarperCollins, London, 1995).

Population and Development Review (quarterly, Population Council, New York).

Sen, Gita, Germain, Adrienne and Chen, Lincoln C. (eds), *Population Policies Reconsidered: Health, Empowerment, and Rights* (Harvard University Press, Boston, Mass., 1994).

PREDICTIONS